For Jay Parini
with respect
and the best wishes

Robt Wrigley
6 April '87

MOON IN A MASON JAR

Poems by Robert Wrigley

University of Illinois Press *Urbana and Chicago*

Publication of this work was supported in part by grants from the
Illinois Arts Council and the National Endowment for the Arts.

This book is printed on acid-free paper.

LIBRARY OF CONGRESS CATALOGING-IN-PUBLICATION DATA

Wrigley, Robert, 1951–

   Moon in a mason jar.

   I. Title.
PS3573.R58M6   1986   811'.54   85-28908
ISBN 0-252-01314-X (alk. paper)

Epigraphs are taken from the following sources:

"A Clear Midnight," by Walt Whitman, *Leaves of Grass & Selected Prose,*
New York: The Modern Library, 1950

Rainer Maria Rilke, Letter to Polish translator Witold von Hulewicz, dated
December 22, 1923, and quoted in *Sonnets,* translated by M. D. Herter Norton,
New York: W. W. Norton & Company, 1942

"Summer Wish," by Louise Bogan, *The Blue Estuaries,* New York: Farrar,
Straus & Giroux, 1968

Some of the poems in this book have appeared previously in the following publications:

"The Beliefs of a Horse," "Mowing," *The American Poetry Review*, Volume 11, Number 3, May/June 1982

"The Skull of a Snowshoe Hare," *The Chariton Review*, Volume 11, Number 2, Fall 1985

"Weaver of Wind," *The Chowder Review*, Number 16/17, Spring–Winter 1981, "Yard Work," Number 10/11, Fall–Winter 1978–79

"Lover of Fire," *Cimarron Review*, Number 68, July 1984 (reprinted here with the permission of the Board of Regents for Oklahoma State University

"A Photo of Immigrants, 1903," *Crab Creek Review*, forthcoming

"Torch Songs," *The Georgia Review*, Volume 29, Number 1, Spring 1985

"Running in Your Sleep," *GiltEdge*, Volume 2, 1981

"The Crèche," *The Kenyon Review*, Volume 7, Number 2, Spring 1985

"The Sound Barrier," *Manhattan Poetry Review*, Number 5, Summer–Fall 1985

"Appalonea," *The Missouri Review*, Volume 5, Number 2, Winter 1981–82

"The Glow," *The Montana Review*, Number 3, 1982, "The Leaning House," "Termites," Number 1, 1979

"Collection," *New England Review & Breadloaf Quarterly*, Volume 6, Number 3, Spring 1984, "Pheasant Hunting," "Star Dust," Volume 8, Number 2, Winter 1985

"Moonlight: Chickens on the Road," *The Ohio Review*, Number 27, 1982

Part 1 of "Aubade for Mothers," *Partisan Review*, Volume 51, Number 3, 1984

"Fireflies," *Quarterly West*, Number 9, Spring–Summer 1979, Part 3 of "Aubade for Mothers," Number 17, Fall–Winter 1983–84, "Heart Attack," Number 13, Fall–Winter 1981–82

"The Owl," *The Seattle Review*, Volume 6, Number 2, Fall 1983

"The Bees," "Nightcrawlers," *Western Humanities Review*, Volume 33, Number 3, Summer 1979

"Heart Attack" & "Mowing" also appeared in the *Anthology of Magazine Verse & Yearbook of American Poetry*, Beverly Hills: Monitor Book Company, 1984

Several of these poems also appeared in the chapbook *The Glow*, Missoula, Montana: Owl Creek Press, 1982

The author would like to express his gratitude to the National Endowment for the Arts for fellowship grants in 1978 and 1984, which enabled him to begin, and to complete, this volume.

CONTENTS

PART ONE

This is thy hour O Soul, thy free flight into the wordless,
Away from books, away from art, the day erased, the lesson done,
Thee fully forth emerging, silent, gazing, pondering the themes thou lovest best,
Night, sleep, death and the stars.

—Whitman

MOONLIGHT: CHICKENS ON THE ROAD

Called out of dream by the pitch and screech,
I awoke to see my mother's hair
set free of its pincurls, springing out
into the still and hurtling air
above the front seat and just as suddenly gone.
The space around us twisted,
and in the instant before the crash
I heard the bubbling of the chickens,
the homely racket they make at all speeds,
signifying calm, resignation, oblivion.

And I listened. All through the slash
and clatter, the rake of steel, shatter of glass,
I listened, and what came
was a blizzard moan in the wind, a wail
of wreckage, severed hoses and lives,
a storm of loose feathers, and in the final
whirl approximating calm, the cluck
and fracas of the birds. I crawled
on hands and knees where a window should
have been and rose uneven

in November dusk. Wind blew
a snow of down, and rows of it quivered along
the shoulder. One thin stream of blood
oozed, flocked in feathers.
This was in the Ozarks, on a road curving miles
around Missouri, and as far as I could
see, no light flickered through the timber,
no mail box leaned the flag
of itself toward pavement, no cars
seemed ever likely to come along.

3

So I walked, circled the darkening disaster
my life had come to, and cried.
I cried for my family there,
knotted in the snarl of metal and glass;
for the farmer, looking dead, half in
and half out of his windshield; and for myself,
ambling barefoot through the jeweled debris,
glass slitting little blood-stars in my soles,
my arm hung loose at the elbow
and whispering its prophecies of pain.

Around and around the tilted car
and the steaming truck, around the heap
of exploded crates, the smears and small hunks
of chicken and straw. Through
an hour of loneliness and fear
I walked, in the almost black of Ozark night,
the moon just now burning into Missouri.
Behind me, the chickens followed my lead,
some fully upright, pecking

the dim pavement for suet or seed,
some half-hobbled by their wounds, worthless wings
fluttering in the effort. The faintest
light turned their feathers phosphorescent,
and as I watched they came on, as though they believed
me some savior, some highwayman
or commando come to save them the last night
of their clucking lives. This, they must have
believed, was the end they'd always heard of,
this the rendering more efficient than the axe,

4

the execution more anonymous than
a wringing arm. I walked on, no longer crying,
and soon the amiable and distracted chattering came
again, a sound like chuckling, or the backward suck
of hard laughter. And we walked
to the cadence their clucking called,
a small boy towing a cloud around a scene
of death, coming round and round
like a dream, or a mountain road,
like a pincurl, like pulse, like life.

1

Maybe you heard them first without knowing,
some silken push and sway behind the walls,
the dim respiration of old and trusty plumbing.
And at first there seemed only a few
stragglers, lost in the maze of city blocks
and alleys, missing flights of half-dozens
daubing their pollen on the window weights,
dying in the no-man's land of dead air
behind the shades.
                    Then one day
you opened the cellar door and heard them
there, befuddled and angry, fallen out
of their intricate hives between the studs.
Soon they were all around you, heaving
in a dark mass upon the houseplants,
bobbing in a top-shaped swarm
above the rich chenille garden of the bedspread.

2

Remember the panic you pushed aside
when they came to you and wove around you
their tight electric air, fluttering
the down on your arms and ears, kissing you
lighter than any man. Remember
your only flinch, minor,
that trapped a bee against your knuckle.
And remember the pain that blossomed
below the skin there, like any true flower.

3

The keeper, in full dress and smoker,
aimed to take a census of the bees, but knew
as soon as you, despite his love,
the emptiness of such a number.
So he flushed them out with a garden hose
and set the cellar awash in tides of the drowned.
A few honeyed drops bled through your walls,
and the bees were gone.
                              That first night
was the stillest you ever heard. The elderly walls
creaked, the toilet murmured for hours.
You thought you'd never sleep in that brittle quiet,
in a house that held its breath
and made you hold yours, thinking
every twitch a bee's dark kiss,
every breath a buzzing.

NIGHTCRAWLERS   *for Paul Zarzyski*

    1
It rains for three days
and out of the ground come worms,
nightcrawlers collared in puddles, caught
too shallow in the mad perc of a cloudburst,
heading for the high country
of sidewalks, the towering crowns of backstreets.
One monster, a foot long, slithers under the back door
and circles in the parched grass of the carpet,
the weave tough as granite, the floorboards tougher.
I pick him up and head for the door.
He can tour the dry moon of the back porch.

    2
Sun flies off a thousand puddles.
From the bedroom window I see corpses covering streets
and sidewalks. They are like limp twigs,
each aimed at dry spots distant as planets.
Inside, my houseguest is gone, over the threshold
or bound for the basement through some chink
in the rug's woof and warp.
                            By noon
the neighborhood is clear, dregs taken up by starlings,
the last of the dead black and dry
as ruined shoes. Water bleeds off into the canyons
and draws, sun gnaws into the garden.
And deep below, the worms begin to rise, ascending
like steam. When I am quiet, I hear them
between drops from eaves and trees.
I hear their soft hiss sifting upward
through the half-moist earth, a dream of dust.

HEART ATTACK

Throwing his small, blond son
into the air, he begins to feel it,
a slow-motion quivering, some part
broken loose and throbbing with its own pulse,
like the cock's involuntary leaping
toward whatever shadow looms in front.

It is below his left shoulder blade,
a blip regular as radar, and he thinks of wings
and flight, his son's straight soar and fall
out of and into his high-held hands.
He is amused by the quick change
on the boy's little face: from the joy

of release and catch, to the near terror
at apex. It is the same with every throw.
And every throw comes without
his knowing. Nor his son's. Again
and again, the rise and fall, like breathing,
again the joy and fear, squeal and laughter,

until the world becomes a swarm of shapes
around him, and his arms
go leaden and prickled, and he knows
the sound is no longer laughter
but wheezing, knows he holds his son
in his arms and has not let him fly

upward for many long moments now.
He is on his knees, as his son stands,
supporting him, the look on the child's face
something the man has seen before:

not fear, not joy, not even misunderstanding,
but the quick knowledge sons

must come to, at some age
when everything else is put aside—
the knowledge of death, the stench
of mortality—that fraction of an instant
even a child can know, when
his father does not mean to leave, but goes.

TERMITES

In one great spasm under the sun
the porch swallows you to the waist.
You stand there, sunk in a mire
of footsteps and disbelief,
blinking, as though you'd been
betrayed by an old friend.
Dust of the half-dry rot floats damply
around you, smelling of roots
and cool soil, mixes with the wind
and is gone.
                    For an instant
you take your short fall for a mineshaft,
the headlong plummet of a heart attack.
Then all your family look on,
crouched on threshold
or peering through bannisters at ground level.
Before their sigh of relief, before
their laughter, and yours,
you see yourself a patient, a prisoner,
a dying man surrounded by doctors,
the hanged man.
                    And you see more:
the intricate combs of the termites,
a trough worn by years of passage
before and behind the door. You kneel
and look closer. The whole underside
of the porch is a perfect mosaic of paths
and wrinkles, the wood's great mark of age.
When your head sinks out of sight,
you can almost hear your family begin to call,
some standing back, others inching out
very close to where you had been.

THE SECRET LIFE IN EVERY STANDING THING

1

It is the secret life in every standing thing,
every live and dead unmoving man
or piano, every car or truck, every wall
and roof and zinging trash can lid.

Vinegar Joe awoke above his restaurant. Downstairs
the water glasses rang like chimes, wine
goblets sang from their clear, immaculate throats.
Joe sat upright, and the bed lurched.

There was a calling in the world, a roar,
a shriek, a growl, a whisper. It was a howl,
a baying. It was lamentations, madness,
all things falling, falling toward the empty center.

The screen pocked outward, instantly gone.
Curtains sucked away, slick as linguini. In a second
Joe was uncovered, his lone sheet
flapping over the room like a lame bird.

Chill came through his bones, all
the hair on his body rose up prickling.
His teeth hammered, and the bed flung
up and dumped him out, the mattress

quick through a window half its size.
Joe skidded over the floor, the close nap
of the carpet burning his fingertips,
the bed frame sunk in the plaster wall.

The springs across the opening sang ululations
to the dead, and Vinegar Joe wept to be there,

hanging in his room by a hand on the radiator pipe
and another knotted in the wobbling coils.

He could see it all, all down the breathing street.
He could not look away, his face mashed against
a circle of springs, his eye that would not close
before the horror. He believed he saw the face of a god.

2

It was the springs that spoke to him, the springs
that saved him. It was the shape of them,
like the storm itself, an infinite coil
of air and debris, a spinning call of curse and prayer.

The cloud came straight for him.
Like a child's top, it grazed the walls
on each side of the street and ricocheted out.
In the building opposite, every floor

collapsed, and Joe saw there was no dust.
All things lighter than the earth were inhaled.
No smoke, no rain, no splinters.
Windows dissolved in a vapor. Joe saw

cars jettisoned, speeding more surely,
accelerating more quickly than their owners ever dreamed.
Parking meters screwed down and exploded
or sank box-deep in the sidewalks.

The restaurant sign rose up before his window,
floating free of the building, yet still aglow
with some miraculous neon. The night was alive
with three dozen tablecloths of gingham.

3

Then there was rain and thunder, the springs
swung away from the window,
and he fell back into his room, still now
but pitching in his tight-spun eyes.

Above him the bed frame hung on the wall,
and the window behind it crashed and flickered.
Lightning lit the room and the world.
A half-moon cut curled from his jaw to his left eye.

Fires came. Natural gas returned
to its severed pipes and ignited, the counting
of the bodies began, and Joe criss-crossed
his neighborhood. A block away was untouched.

Now night was woven with its human noises,
sirens and bullhorns, rev and grunt
of backhoe and crane, all the man-made alarms
and implements of hope, insubstantial and frail.

Vinegar Joe sat in his restaurant, behind
the wheel of a '59 Ford. He found a tablecloth,
folded it double, and spread it on the dash.
He found a wine goblet with only a chipped base

and three bottles of chianti balanced on a slanted shelf,
all cleanly uncorked. He crossed the wires
of the starter switch, tuned in music on the radio,
and waited for the light of morning.

It was what he believed he could do.
Then, idly, his half-empty goblet held

on the curve of the steering wheel,
he began tracing the moist crystal edge.

A column of music, a constant note
from deep in the breath-blown throat of the goblet,
and the hair on Joe's body came up electric.
The car radio joined in, and the night

was clotted with an otherworldly singing,
sirens and diesel bawlings blocked out.
Beneath him, Joe felt the seat of the Ford
awaken, a fluttery, spun-wire warbling that throbbed

in the cut on his face, the half-moon scored down
his temple and cheek, as though it held there
some invisible, crystalline shell, in which
he could hear an ocean of breathing.

THE BELIEFS OF A HORSE

In the field out back
there are some sheep, fat
and unsheared; two heifers;
and a pinto horse, his spots
like a map of continental drift.
One day soon a man will come
with his pistol and his high-backed
truck and take away the sheep
and the heifers, leaving
around the gate the steaming piles
of viscera, blood gathering
at the low point in a slow
and thickening rivulet.
The fence rails will fill up
with ravens. The air will throb
with bluebottle flies.
While all this time the horse
will merely stand, waiting for his
day on the trail,
as still as he can, monumental,
barely breathing, believing
among the flickers of leaves,
the slow-passing cloud shadows,
that he is lost
on the earth's great sea, that he is an island
on which the breeze quietly laps
and the sun passes by in its current,
the fence a near horizon
that will someday break wide with sails.

LOVER OF FIRE

1

Musk-wet, hay smells, the acrid sweet
aroma of horse dung. It is night.
The watchman one time at ten o'clock passes
then slouches in his office under the grandstand
and sleeps. He keeps his radio on
the all-night talk and squabble show
from St. Louis. When his phone rings,
the caller must believe no one could sleep
through such caterwauls and hollers.

Now I scale the fence, chain link
and well above my head, the last foot
strung aslant with barbed wire,
dropping as I have these twenty nights
to move among the stables like a spirit,
a presence almost acknowledged
by the low nickers here, a head-thrown snort
or snuffle there, and everywhere the breathing,
huge and dark, hot and damply sexual.

I come to them as a dream.
My hand on their flanks calls forth
a twitch—quick, insignificant, powerful.
Imagine so much precision
within your flesh, like a mountain
aware of a sliver of stone,
the night sky winking its feeblest star
across a billion to this place. All night
I watch to make out its whisper: it is *fire*.

2

Hay transcends itself. From my lighter
it leaps and stretches, bright
as the jockeys' silks, all the empty end
stalls quickly glaring. Already in
the low shining, the step-clop and whinnying,
I know the terror unrolls with the smoke.
One by one they begin wrenching,
eye whites flashing in the flame light,
kicking horror-driven at the hard stall doors.

Outside among the trailers I am hidden.
The watchman runs past, his keys
ringing like parade regalia. He is saying
to the stars "Oh Jesus God
Oh Jesus God . . . " And inside, the horses
are wild, the supple necks twisting,
pampered hoofs clattering the gray
unyielding wood: the many stallions,
the colts, the ghostly dreams of mares.

VOLUNTEERS

Siren over snow, blare
and howl of it over the year's
worst blizzard. I am up
crashing into clothes
and furniture, still
tugging on my gloves as I run
and slog the single snow-clogged block
to where the night glows gold.

It is the community center,
poor old false-fronted, hollow-toned
hall, now ablaze at eaves
and ridge pole, burning
from the top down, like a candle
or a flare, a campfire
planted in the pit
of winter night.
Del Heywood kicks in the front door,
calls for help. "Let's
get the snooker table, boys!"
A few of us gather near
the entrance. Even in the winter
chill the heat is fierce, the fire
now drawing through the open door,
exploding through the roof tins,
turning for one long moment
this blizzard to a snow of sparks.

Del peers in, up
at the rafters filigreed
in flames, and we all walk
back across the street
to stand among the gathering crowd

in front of the Rexall,
in the lee of the wind,
in a silence like none of us
has ever heard.

We let her go that night.
Old hall of silly dances,
bingo parlor, scene of every
meeting no one remembers so well
as where, now that the new
school is in, with a gym
and a theater, many clean
linoleumed classrooms,
and a flat roof already sagging.
By the time the false front falls,
everyone adult who could heave
through two feet of snow
is huddled at the curb
across the street, volunteers
in this cold and snowy place, warming
to the fall of ancient timbers,
gold on every quiet face.

MOWING

Sleepy and suburban at dusk,
I learn again the yard's
geometry, edging around the garden
and the weedy knots of flowers, circling
trees and shrubs, giving
a wide berth to the berry patch,
heavy and sprawled out of its bounds.
Shoving such a machine
around a fairway of dandelions,
it is easy to feel absurd.
The average lawn, left alone
one hundred years, could become
a hardwood forest. An admirable project.
Still I carry on, following week on week
the same mowing pattern, cutting edges,
almost sprinting the last narrow swaths.
And tonight, as I mow over
the bushels of fallen peaches,
sending pits soaring over the neighbors' fences,
seems hardly any different.
But on one crooked march I walk
across the thin hidden hole
to a yellowjacket hive. The blade pulls
them up from their deep sweet chamber
just as my bare legs go by.

A bee lands heavily,
all blunder and revenge, and the sting
is a quick embrace and release,
like the dared kid's run and touch
of a blind man. I'm blind now
with the shock and pain of it,
howling in a sprint toward the house,

the mower flopped on its side, wild blade loose
in the darkening air.
                         Later,
the motor sputtered quiet, starved by tilt,
I'm back in the twilight,
a half-dozen stings packed in wet tobacco,
carrying a can of gasoline, a five-foot torch.
The destruction is easy: shove can
slow to entranceway lip, pull
back and light torch, use torch
to tip can. One low *whump* and it's over.
A few flaming drones flutter out and fall.
Stragglers, late returners, cruise
wide circles around the ruins.
In the cool September night they fly
or die. In the morning I finish my chores.

All the way to winter the blackened hole
remains. On Christmas Eve a light
late snow covers it and all
the lawn's other imperfections: crabgrass
hummocks, high maple roots,
the mushroom-laden fairy ring that defies
obliteration and appears every spring
more visible than ever. Standing
in the window, the scent
of pine powerful around me,
the snap of wood undoing itself in the stove,
I wonder at this thin and cold
camouflage, falling,
gradually falling over what has gone
and grown before. And I hear
that other rattle and report, that engine

driven by another fire. I think of a gold
that is sweet and unguent, a gold
that is a blaze of years behind me.
I hear wind in its regular passes
blowing across the roof,
feel in my legs a minute and icy tingling,
as though I have stood too long
in one place or made again another wrong step,
as though the present itself
were a kind of memory, coiled, waiting,
dying to be seen from tomorrow.

YARD WORK

I am seven years old
when a neighborhood maniac kills my dog
with a pitchfork. It is mid-
May. My father and I carry the corpse
in a red wagon, wrap it in
a bedspread, and bury it deep
in the backyard.
                All summer long
with a number 2 shovel my father nips
at that tilted yard, and I dream at night
he struggles with its grassy edge, to lift it
and snap it like a mussed blanket.
In the morning, though, there is only the regular
chink and *slop* of his hopeless shovel.

I dream he must do this. I dream
he is digging the maniac's monstrous grave,
that he will slit that fat man's belly
with the tines of his own pitchfork.

One day, after school begins, I come over the hill
to see the yard sodded and level
as slow-rising water, a neat white cross
on the dog's grave. My father sits
on his heels, cradling his shovel
like a dangerous weapon, sipping lemonade
from a metal canteen.
                I have never seen
anyone so tired. And if he smiled through
his dusty face then, I've forgotten.
He said over his shoulder nothing special,
but walked to the house stooped and sore,
loaded with the freight of a good man.

24

PART TWO

We are the bees of the invisible. We frantically plunder the visible
of its honey, to accumulate it in the great golden hive of the invisible.

—Rilke

FIREFLIES

Now there are no fireflies. Once
there were, and we caught them,
our white sweaters glinting
in the dusk, chasing after children.
They were like that, like children
or the very old, doddering in slow flight.
We'd charge any flash and wait
at arm's length for another. And always,
there was. Once we kept them
in an unwashed honey jar, two dozen
snagged and flickering on the oozy sides.
Carefully we plucked them away and wrote
with the smears of their phosphorescence
our names on a stone wall,
then afterwards licked our fingers,
and they were sweet and golden.

for Hugh Nichols

The man believes in blood, in the dog
beside him so remarkably alive, keen
in his eyes and up-pricked ears,
miraculously not bolting, loosed
from the long year's chain-link kennel.
He believes in blood, in his heart
drumming like a grouse, the dog
out front still as earth and holding,
blood in them all holding, still
as the dog is still, the man,
the birds.
        We might leave them
as they are now, frozen
in the thistle-cluttered gully,
below wheat stubble, the noisy arcs
of grasshoppers like a cartoon model
of the cosmos. It could be a painting,
fall gold and salmon sky at dawn,
framed and lit from above,
mounted in the den
by the blue-black steel and sweet oil
redolence of the gun rack. But how
account for the blood, then,
knowing in this scene it is not posed
but poised, that it must, before we go,
resume its motions inevitable as sun-
light or stars.
        Four birds flush,
one falls, and the gun shatter tumbles
over the valley like a stone,
like the sound a star might make
in its plummet, or the thistle,
wind-blown, to the smallest,

most sensitive ears. The dog
cavorts, retrieves, his soft mouth
innocent. A smear of blood
crosses the man's hand and jacket,
a brush stroke he understands.

THE SKULL OF A SNOWSHOE HARE

I found it in the woods, moss-mottled,
hung at the jaws by a filament
of leathery flesh. We have painted it
with Chlorox, bleached it
in that chemical sun, boiled loose
the last tatters of tissue,
and made of it an heirloom,
a trophy, a thing that lasts, death's
little emissary to an eight-year-old boy.

What should it mean to us now
in its moon-white vigil on the desk?
Light from the hallway makes it loom
puffball brilliant, and I look.
For no good reason but longing
I am here in your room,
straightening the covers, moving a toy,
and lightly stroking your head,
those actions I have learned to live by.

If we relish the artifacts of death,
it's for a sign that life goes on
without us. On the mountain snows
we've seen the hare's limited hieroglyphics,
his signature again and again
where we've skied. And surely
he has paused at our long tracks there,
huddled still as moonlight, and tested
for our scents long vanished in that air.

We live and die in what we have left.
For all the moon glow of that bone
no bigger than your fist, there is more

light in the way I touch you
when you're sleeping: the little electric sparks
your woolen blankets make together,
the shape of your head clear
to my hand in the half-light,
and this page, white as my bones, and alive.

Your hands flesh it out. It fins hard
through rapids and years, and I
can see on your faces—quiet, clear—
how the flesh still works, and you believe.

TOUCHING THE CARP

They looked reptilian in the lake's mud
edges, and we knew there were some who ate
the bony flesh. We meant only to touch
them, the heavily cross-hatched backs and sides,
the blue and silver bellies upturned
in the half-gone light at Rend Lake.

I wonder now if we ever meant to fish the lake,
a prairie reservoir dense with weeds and mud.
Her father came to the window when I turned
in his driveway at eight
o'clock that morning. The rusty sides
of my old car had not seen the touch

of sponge or chamois in years. But touch
was all our aim, and Rend Lake,
any lake, would do—its dark side
roads, its impassable mud
that kept away the crowds. We had eight
long hours of love ahead, I had just turned

seventeen, and she turned
to kiss me just outside the straining touch
of her father's field of vision. We kissed, we ate
lunch, we baited and fished the lakes
of ourselves, played in the sweet, salt mud
flesh is at seventeen, in the back seat, side by side.

Just before we left, we walked the near side
of Rend Lake, held our clammy hands, and turned
to see them: in swirls of mud
and water, sodden shore grasses, a mass of carp touched

together, boiling at the lake's
shallow edge, a roiling sculpture of eight

or a dozen. There were some who ate
them, but we only knelt alongside
those trash fish, so lovely in the drab lake
debris, so graceful in their weaving turns,
so intricately coiled and lightly touching:
we meant to touch them as we knelt in that mud.

And all eight or ten or more, at their slow turns
sidelong in the shallows, were lovingly touched and touched,
then swam for the lake, leaving trails of amber mud.

THOSE RICHES

The week after your father left
you still carried his note in your wallet,
and on the night before the bank
said they'd come for the car,
we were on our way to St. Louis,
our last dime in the gas tank, and you
every way you could find
abusing that sad family sedan,
pounding the dash for the radio it lacked,
shifting without the clutch
and wringing from its feeble six
every stinking, oil-ridden mile per hour.
Down the long hill past the Catholic cemetery,
under the dead viaduct
and into the bottom lands we rolled.
You spoke of jobs you might have soon
at this or that plant or refinery,
smoked my cigarettes, thought
you'd save up for a car and a tattoo.
Through the banks of smog,
the swampland haze, great flames rose
above the foundries and steel mills,
and there was nothing in school
so bright. It was Saturday night,
and you would never go back, not ever.

We found our way to Gaslight Square
and drove slowly down its streets.
You refused to acknowledge the sidewalk crowds,
the soul and blues, the smack jazz
seething from the nightclubs.
At the last bright reaches we were stalled
by traffic, and a whore in hot pants

called from a Laundromat doorway. Sugar,
she sang, and came outward. She walked
to your window, leaned her breasts on your arm,
grinned, and you turned and spat in her face.

What you could not accomplish that night
a handful of outraged, high-heeled prostitutes could.
They kicked at our fenders, spit
with amazing accuracy through our windows.
And with what you claimed to have seen and known
as a blackjack, one leering redhead
bashed in the windshield, turning all
its clear expanse to a sagging honeycomb
of safety glass, before the traffic opened
and we were on our way half blind
into the diesel-scented city night.

Could that have been what we were after,
that joy, those riches
reeling from destruction?
Ten blocks farther on we stopped
and forced the whole window out, down
onto the dash and floor and front seat,
then drove home with the summer highway
wind in our faces, laughing,
sitting in a gravel of glass
that flashed under streetlights,
in the full of the moon, like a carload of diamonds.

TORCH SONGS

I would speak of that grief
perfected by the saxophone, the slow
muted trombone, the low unforgettable cornet.
Theirs were the paths we followed
into the sexual forest, the witch's spellbound cabin,
the national anthems of longing.

Rhythm is the plod of the human heart,
that aimless walker down deserted streets
at midnight, where a tavern's neon keeps the pulse.
A horn man licks the blood
in tow, heavy and smooth,
and a song is in the veins like whiskey.

Does it matter then that men have written
the heartbreaks women make hurt?
that Holiday and Smith sang for one
but to the other? Or is everything equal
in the testimonies of power and loss?
Is the writer the body, the singer the soul?

Now your eyes are closed,
your head leaned back and off to one side.
Living is a slow dance you know
you're dreaming, but the chill at your neck
is real, the soft, slow breathing
of someone you will always love.

STAR DUST

That crooning they swooned for, all the moons in June
and sweet talk of broken hearts forever: the man
in his apartment hears buses hiss and roar
below his window, a television set next door,
but listens to Dorsey and Sinatra on the phonograph,
feels a quiet settle over his flesh, the laugh
of muted trumpets coming down soft as rain.

He could look for hours into the room's
empty spaces—the blind stares, his father called them.
And he knows it is melancholy, a nameless
yearning not for his own youth, but for that famous
eon of his father's, a blind time
before one war or another, and all those fine
fine tunes that lull him now to dream

without sleep. He believes a song
is a dream, memory nothing but a long
lyric he'll never completely know.
He thinks of his parents, years ago,
huddled on the old Ford's hood, wrapped
in a woolen blanket and watching the lake water lap
the shore under star shine. On the radio a song

from Dorsey and Sinatra rang the perfect omen.
Tonight is what they could not know, when
he would ache with his nothing, grow still
below the weight of what is empty, all that any song will
do. Like the star beaming outward past its death,
the buses and the rain he loses track of,
the music comes and goes, and he remembers again.

THE SOUND BARRIER

1

We were in our beds or daydreaming
out a window in school,
or we were simply running, the fleet
childish joy of motion through a still, dusty field.
It was silence that shattered.

In 1961 I was dreaming baseball
when the bomb of air blew up. The bed
lurched, I raised my head to hear the windows
clattering in their frames, my mother's trinkets ringing.
And when I settled back into sleep, the room fell away.
There was a rush of dreams like stars,
the rustle of bedclothes trailing off.

2

At the end of its road in Illinois
my father's house sat cracking in the cold.
A light from the kitchen window shone
a rectangle in the snow, my father
at the table yawning toward work.
The sweep of his hair left a mark on the window.
He leaned to see. A high flash
crossed the sky, the brief faded wash of its roar.

This is for you in that airplane, the exhilaration
you must have felt, my father cursing you
for everyone on earth.

THE GLOW

1

Above the playground, from the hung-out
highest limb of a creaking, leafless elm,
the bee hive breathed all summer long,
a low sizzle high up. It grew
like the mound of mud thrown out
by a crawdad, hurled up
on wind around the thick and empty limb,
a great bronze breast hung sweet
above the faces of children.

The sky was its own
electric fence. Every high and wobbly
fly ball fell from its arc
as though swatted down, an egg shoved off
the sky's blue table. And birds
gave the whole tree a berth,
even the woodpecker, who strayed
from his place among locusts
to patter a while the elm's infested trunk

and flew away wild in swoops
from the dark swarm
the hive hauled out to halt him.
Only the wind moved high in timber,
its hiss across leaves
a harmony to the bee's wiry buzzing.
Still they sent out sentries,
who fought the wind's tug and toss
and wound up lost, stung

out from sinking their skewers
all across an enemy's invisible flank.
On such days, the hive heaving

overhead, teachers called
in their students, and from the windows
all afternoon small gazes flared
hard, wondering if this day would be
the last of the bees' lording over,
the high hold held finally in check.

2

Windows razzed with grit
and the great bowl of the playground
lay below the school, overflowing
with dust. All around
darkened to storm, and teachers
reviewed the choreographies
of disaster. Then came rain,
whipped in the sky to froth,
spattering onto glass its

million small scars. Here
and there a pane gave out
and the school sucked hard the cold
air. Halls filled with
files of frightened children,
rambling lunchless to the deep
and quiet cafeteria, some dazzled
silent, others sobbing, whimpering
for father, mother, sunshine.

They sat below the storm's
unmuffled engine, and when the walls
around them held they began
to laugh. The room roared
with the voices of children, voices

thrown high and excited by the wind
and their own clattering hearts.
Among such laughter and the scoots of stools,
every child forgot about the bees.

3

Every one but the one who lived
next door, whose whole summer was spent
lolling in the cool near woods
and the playground's dusty spaciousness,
who daily gauged by his upheld thumb
the hive's expansion,
whose bedroom window caught every morning
the first early dronings.
This one hid among coats and sweaters

and the day's hollow clang
of lunch pails. Knowing
he had only until the rolls
were taken, he slipped out soon behind
his classmates, dodging teachers
in their last-minute swings, and walked
out into rain and chaos, the wind
aswirl with water and leaves,
with mud and birds and everything

but bees. With his left shoulder
he leaned downhill into the playground,
the school behind him paling to a hulk,
a shadow, before it was completely gone.
He looked down around him
for the minor landmarks a child
remembers, having studied this land

more carefully than any
textbook. But old grasses

swooned with the weight of weather.
There was nowhere a sign
he could sight from, no hummock of weed
that tripped him one day, no bare
mark of mud where second base
or third had received his slide.
Now the slant of the land itself
seemed wrong, and he sat
in the thunder and rain, and waited.

4

Among the stone rumbles of the storm,
wind yelping through trees and brush,
he heard the first low pop of the trunk
giving way, a wooden spoon
broken under water. The soft
mush of old heartwood sputtered,
quiet cardboard crackling, and then,
while the sparse crown swung silent
in its fall, there were only the sounds of storm.

It appeared black above him,
a wooden claw holding a hunk
of honey, workers, and wax.
He could hear the hive's
respiration, a million wings worrying
close and pungent air. Down
like some prehistoric bird it came,
from a Saturday movie and nightmare,
and he covered his face with his arms,

waited for the yank or crush.
But he was suddenly swaddled in tree.
All around him leaves and branches
closed in, nipping light and sharp his face
and arms, sending him a foot
in the air on the trunk's concussion,
and dumping at his feet, on his feet,
an offering of honey and comb,
gold and pearl all across him.

To his left he saw the ground a mass
of bees imbedded in their lives,
lifting up dizzy toward their deaths.
He saw against wet bark the queen
sealed in a dollop, still and perfect
as an amulet. A few drones grazed
his anointed body, as though
he were a large and bounteous flower.
He rose and walked into the rain.

        5

For a long while he wandered lost,
until the school rose up before him.
He walked through the door and passed
down halls littered with glass
and papers, slowly,
his feet clinging in their golden boots,
and descended the stairs
to be once again among the others,
children, teachers, who only then
noticed his absence and turned
to the door, uttered one low cry,
and stopped. The eyes

of every adult and child
turned to the figure in the doorway,
his clothes frayed, heavy with rain,
his face a smear of small bleeding cuts
and drops of honey, winking
in the lights like iridescent scabs.

From his shoes amber puddles flowed
outward. All up and down
his legs was a fresco of bees,
mementos, souvenirs
fastened to a plaque and varnished.
The room lay before him
like a photograph, every face caught
in the moment's quick shutter.
He will remember them that way,

frozen in their stares,
peering up at the miracle of him,
not knowing whether
the look in his eyes
was terror or the transfix
of high wind and venom. He will remember
himself in their eyes, the look
that will not go away
for years and years

of his life as someone partly other
than human, removed, as necessary
and dangerous as a bee,
as chosen and blessed as any survivor.
In the halls and on the playground,
on the streets, he will feel the glow of gold

they have seen around him, hear the whirr
they heard that day, as bees
came to life in his matted hair.

PART THREE

Speak out the wish like music, that has within it
The horn, the string, the drum pitched deep as grief.

—Louise Bogan

A PHOTO OF IMMIGRANTS, 1903

You could cry at their faces.
Father forces a smile
and Mother looks into the lens
as she must have looked for weeks
into the distances of the Atlantic.
The infant dangles her feet
against sack cloth, and the boy,
four maybe, looks up at his hand
in his father's, as though surprised
to find it there. Or perhaps
the look on his face is pain, his father
holding on too hard. The ship in back
loads for the return to Danzig:
crates of pencils, pistons, bolts of linen.
By its first moorage, these four will be on their way
to Cleveland or Chicago. They will have seen
the Statue of Liberty and looked past it
for the world. They will have sweltered
on the train all through Ohio
and August.
            And in five years
they will write to their friends in Cracow,
enclose a few dollars, a new and cheerful photograph.
Father will tell in his most earnest prose
the ordeal of the Atlantic passage
and the ecstacy of arrival.
He will have himself removing his hat
and blowing kisses to the city, laughing
and clapping with his fellows. And that night
he will mail his letter, walking slowly
to the post office with his daughter.
He will hear two men there speak again
of the great lake to the north of the city

and vow to visit it when there is time.
He will stop and tell his daughter of his plans.
She will nod and walk on, walking oddly
on the sides of her feet, hoping
he will soon let go of her hand,
speak English, or loosen
at least his fierce and powerful grip.

THE CRÈCHE

It survived the loud, jostling train
from Baden to Berlin, and the heave
and slant, the pitch, pivot and lean
of the bad boat to New York.
She held it to her in a hatbox
stuffed with husks, all across steerage
and Pennsylvania, down the slow road
of the Ohio River to Cairo
and up the dirt tracks and coal-
paved paths to Frankfort, Illinois,
her sudden husband, her life.
She was mined for the children
in her, one daughter, then another,
a short seam, quick to clay,
and not a single son to save them.

But each December found her unfolding
from their sheaths the pale
figures from Dresden: Holy Mother, mild
worker in wood, stock reclined
and ruminant, the infant peering skyward
through His upheld hands. And through the years
we have come to know this story,
how starved, buried on scrip to the company store,
the miner came coal-hearted home,
winter just begun, his daughters already asleep,
and the crèche below a sprig of pine.
How blind in the peripheral light, unhelmeted
to rage, he crushed the manger and the tiny Lord
in his blackened right hand,
spat the word *woman* in her face,
and left that night and never returned.

There the story ends, but for one daughter
who married, bore another, who bore
a son, who fathered three boys—two that survived—
and one that passed on the crèche,
the Holy Mother, husband, endlessly
sleepy stock, and the gap since then gathered round,
its eloquent absence,
its grip more powerful than any man's.

There may have been a time when
your name went unnoticed: Amethyst,
Hortensia, and Emerald Maisie Hopes
were your chums, your names
sparkling off the page like so much paste
and silver plate. The Chinese
say you are not truly dead
until the last soul who knew your name
forgets it. Somehow we misplaced yours
against remarkable odds: a name
like a bird that sings its own,

or conjures up music
and hard fruit. Winesap, Golden
Delicious, the loud applause of wind
in the dry leaves of autumn.
But not a single shining image
of the human face. Grandfather's
grandmother, anyone we both knew
is dead now, and rooting
through certificates and microfilm
we've found every vital statistic but your face.

So I talk, and your name
is the only answer. Appalonea. Apotheosis
of appellations, a plum of pure sound.
Apollo, Apollonius, Apollinaire.
The great Johnny Appleseed
who gave us a peachy cider, a press,
and a pint of apple jack. I'm drunk
in the swirl of your name, the way
it applies to everything I see:

that strong grayish horse
across the field: Appaloosa,
a portrait but not a picture,
a prize, a poem, Appalonea.

WEAVER OF WIND

Her hands go on in the dark,
tatting doilies over quilts
and blankets, patient arabesques
of sleep and fine string.
She follows a pattern
borrowed from a garden spider.

In the morning she remembers
blindness, come closer
with every hook of her needle,
the shuttle's each loud pass.
Her world moves in a milky blur.

She remembers too the last months
and what they have taken from her:
the loom, the sewing machine
with its sweet creaky treadle,
all her needles.

Now she sits in her chair
on the front porch, knotting
and unknotting the wind,
tying in labyrinthine bows
the strings of her apron, braiding
her hair to a sleek, white rope.

And after work her children come
to do their unraveling, to help
with her dinner. They hurry
along with their knives
and hot plates, fret over
the clock and the dust on the furniture.
They do all they believe they can.

They kiss lightly the top of her head
and leave her washing vegetables,
not noticing the sift of her hands
through lacey carrot tops,
her fingers swirling in the colander,
tracing stars.

You're running, not
the breathy strides
of a woman from her
body's relentless spreading,
but running for your life
out of dream that lopes
over years like low hurdles.
Among the breweries
and workers' bars, the dark
stadium, the loading docks
thundering across the highway
below you, you're running
out of a past as quick as it is
brutal, relentless as tomorrow
and the treadmill you sleep on,
the sad race every night
has come to be.
                    Of him
you remember only his small,
thick frame, his glasses,
the wheeze of his chase
that sounded every breath
like his last. You remember him
gaining. You were young then.
Today you'd never keep up
his pace, but that night
he kept on, and so did you,
dropping first your purse
then your long, worn coat
as obstacles along the causeway,
tripping him up in the darkness
and making him angry.
It was his shouting that caused

your crying, your calling
to your mother, who
for all the time she could not afford
for love held you long until light
and long nights after.

Now you read how safe it is
to be frightened, and you are.
No one ever chased me
with death on his hands, rape,
choking desperate and refusing to go
down. No one saw me
working beyond my age, gave me
ruin as a legacy, hope as a cause
already lost.
              Running as you will
until memory gives out,
there's little help a son can offer.
Only this: all breath gets stirred
in the lungs. The cry of a baby
can lapse into the softest sleep,
the rasps of lovers
sometimes go on and on.
And lovers will lose their easy motions
when they pass mirrors, when
they see in regrettable lights
the long, long ways they've come,
frightened, sad, and lonely.
But some of them are still
caught up in each other,
running away from the spouse
we must all lie down with,
and toward the other,

those years and moments between,
the motions of the body
and the soul, running.

THE LEANING HOUSE

for my grandmother

Everything leans north
where wind splits
the corner of the house.
Storm nights, cellophane covers
on windows swell in and out,
shirts filled and emptied of breath.
Gravy, dumplings in their bowls,
milk and coffee in cups: each leaves
a tilted ellipse above the old table,
and every year another thin wedge of matchbook
slips under the south legs.
Behind us, bottles in the icebox pitch
back as though they would lean
out of reach, and we eat,
half of us straining past our laps
to our dishes, others drawing back
every bite with a push of the legs.
For the woman who lives here
the world is the uneven place, her home
as flat as a frozen lake. She walks
these halls and creaking rooms
with a balance blossomed in habit, leaning
between us one hot dish after another,
eyeing all our plates and smiling.
We eat, and keep holding on.

AUBADE FOR MOTHERS

1   The Ritual of Expulsion and Yearning

I am alone in the nursery corridor,
moving window to window,
perusing each child's melon face.
I see my own in her bassinet
of aluminum and glass, my own
faint in the finger-clouded pane.
The swell to my abdomen is gentler
today. There are spasms, intermittent,
expected, the ritual of expulsion and yearning.

The first memory is presence, first
sensation is loss. These are shapes,
colors, blood-muffle or chorus of winds.
In his swaddling before me, someone's
child flinches and feints, ducks
his wizened little face quick
behind his hands. What figures
can he see in his dreams? what terrors?
what sanctuaries of flesh and bone?

The nurses have cuffed my daughter's hands,
the slash of her newborn nails.
But for now she sleeps peacefully, open-mouthed,
lightly drooling. When I lean away
from the window, I see her
through the mark my forehead has left,
a fog of my own making,
through which she outwardly sails
on the certain and ritual waves.

2   A Cloth of Reunion and Love

Now they are all asleep, my friends
and their children, my sons, my daughter
and my husband, weary of so much elation.
I have waited for this instant. I came back
to the living room, banked the fire,
and began to sit, to stare
out at the common air of all our lives,
the night our breaths have woven
into fabric, a cloth of reunion and love.

The air breathed out by beloved sleepers
is like a dance of souls
or a system of weathers—storm clouds,
clear skies: I see now that the dew is no more
than an aura made plain every day,
the pure energy of children,
a fog of heat rising from the bed rolls.
How strange it is, a mother's breath
coming from one I knew as a child!

Her sleep sound is a soft wet rasp,
her daughter's just the same. Her son
rumbles like me: it will always be spring
in his life, short storms, wild greenings.
I listen to her breathing, my friend's,
and I am lulled. I should be
asleep too. But I can't sleep now.
I am a mother myself, there is tomorrow,
and now the night comes down with its rag.

3   Aubade for Mothers and Their Lives

The seconds screamed, the minutes writhed
toward midnight. But now the room
grows back its familiar objects,
the suck and wash of the respirator is less,
my mother's sad dying body still lives.
At their homes my brothers are
readying themselves for my call,
and I feel like dancing, like singing:
an aubade for mothers and their lives.

My joy is not strange: we are alone,
my mother and I. She cannot speak,
I won't. But I think to myself how
the tubes from her body dangle and rise
like *ivy*. It is a pun
she would be pleased by. Death
when it comes will be a man.
He will nod to me, deferential, and, waving,
Mother will leave this grave to the earth.

This morning, it is April, the crocuses glisten
dewy under the sun, the seasonal birds
babble. Something like my mother's
soul wavers in the air above her body.
Suddenly I know the moment
of my conception, a morning like this!
I long for my husband, cuffing the children
at home. And now I am laughing:
I think that I will never be alone.

THE OWL   *for Phyllis Wright*

I was young, and leaned
against the gray boards, almost sleeping.
Newly weaned from the drill and splash,
the chamber pot's porcelain contingency,
I knew just enough of darkness
and nightsounds, the musky aroma
of the outhouse, to doze there,
my nightdress gathered round me like a flourish.

When the owl lit, I knew it was God.
My first look from the door's
slim crack was proof: white
and blazing with moonlight, it lifted outward and made
in two great and silent wing flaps
the chicken house, dark and unclucking
across the yard. The black eyes rolled over
the lawn like searchlights.

Again and again it flew across
the still world, silent as a star.
Until once, as it left its perch above me,
it tilted and came instantly down
on my yearling gray cat. Just a flash
of talon, a gnarled leg of amber,
and both were gone, the winging silent as ever
across hayfields, the pulse of wings

a silver trail into trees. I ran inside
and shivered in my bed until daylight. Since
that day, I have wondered
how I came to be there, sleepy
and desperate in the stillness. The cat
likewise, yawning in its moonlight

meander after rodents and moths.
And the bird, the snowy owl,
winging effortless as breath.

Little girls rose then, and padded
out blinking, scratching, unafraid. And cats
have always been the denizens of farmscapes.
It is a world removed now
from my daughters, who still wander from their rooms,
sleepy and tidal, indoors, wakened by the moon.
I lie in my bed and listen, remembering.

Then I sleep, the dream taking me
away on great white wingbeats,
regular as moonrise, nightly as letting go.

MOON IN A MASON JAR

It was what you might as well wish for,
blue-in-the-face, pipe-dreamer.
Money taunts, another year
is gone by and still you're in that old coat,
those over-hauled dresses, your face
hand-tooled to a frown
while you dun by phone the other bad debtors.

Rue the day the fourth child was born,
rue worse the day it started.
Your hands are crabbed in wash water,
nails ravaged. And there is no sense
in happiness despite it all,
no glad release when, sweat-soaked,
you stack the last jar of fruit
on the pantry shelves and stand back to see them,
the yolky peaches, wine cherries,
the cool lunar lobes of the pears,
and the accompaniment each lid makes
as it pings and seals itself tight.

796.8
FRE

Frew, Katherine

Gladiators

23140

$24.95

DATE	ISSUED TO
	Willie
	Jacob
	John
	Hameed
	nanvl
	Skyler

DATE	ISSUED TO
	Cara
	Skylan
	Nathan